THE NEW DESIGN

shelves and bookcases

repisas y libreros

étagères et bibliothèques

regale und bücherregale

Authors
Fernando de Haro & Omar Fuentes

Editorial Design & Production

EDITORES PUBLISHERS

Project Managers
Carlos Herver Díaz | Ana Teresa Vázquez de la Mora | Laura Mijares Castellá

Coordination
Ana Lydia Arcelus Cano | Cristina Gutiérrez Herce | Alejandra Martínez-Báez Aldama

Prepress Coordination
José Luis de la Rosa Meléndez

Copywriter
Víctor Hugo Martínez

English translation
Fionn Petch

French translation
Isadora Mora

German translation
Claudia Wondratschke

THE NEW DESIGN
SHELVES AND BOOKCASES • REPISAS Y LIBREROS • ÉTAGÈRES ET BIBLIOTHÈQUES • REGALE UND BÜCHERREGALE

© 2013, Fernando de Haro & Omar Fuentes
AM Editores S.A. de C.V.
Paseo de Tamarindos 400 B, Suite 109, Col. Bosques de las Lomas, C.P. 05120, México D.F.
Tel. & Fax 52 (55) 5258 0279
ame@ameditores.com www.ameditores.com

ISBN 978-607-437-253-3

Printed in China.

INDEX | ÍNDICE

INTRODUCTION
INTRODUCCIÓN
INTRODUCTION
EINLEITUNG

Books and decorative objects alike are an essential part of our everyday lives. The former enclose our history and the whole cultural universe that surrounds us from antiquity up to the present day; the latter reflect our taste and personality, possess material or sentimental value, and endow our home with meaning and symbolism. Both are silent companions which also transport us to imaginary universes where we can recall a journey, a country, a culture, a personal story.

At the same time, books are increasingly becoming design objects in themselves: items that are valued highly not only for their content, but for their appearance, typography, color, publishing house and other features that sometimes makes them highly sought-after objects for demanding collectors. They share this value with decorative objects or items that, regardless of their origin, size, subject matter or material are transformed into details that delight our gaze.

This makes it no coincidence that in interior design and décor these two elements demand a special, prominent position where they can be enjoyed. With this in mind, shelves and bookcases are the ideal elements to serve this purpose, whether as accessories exclusively designed for a new space, or those acquired later because of their individual qualities and added to a particular room.

The shelves and bookcases holding all these pieces should show them off at their best, while at the same time serving to embellish a space in their own right. It should also be borne in mind that their arrangement may reflect the particular function they are assigned: for frequent consultation and reading; ornament or decoration; and finally, exhibition or protection of collector's items.

Once this has been defined, a number of elements may come together that make these components much more attractive in a given setting. It is possible to play with different materials, forms and colors as much as the situation requires, since their presence may emerge in spaces designed in conjunction with the architectural space, as technically more demanding constructive elements; or on the contrary be complete in the space with a simplicity that is much more precise, and almost imperceptible.

In this way, together with the right lighting, specific placing, a personal style that highlights them and individual creativity or taste, these elements become unique visual finishes that are full of personality and character.

Tanto los libros como los objetos decorativos forman parte indispensable de nuestra vida cotidiana. En los primeros se encuentra nuestra historia y también todo el universo cultural que nos rodea desde la antigüedad hasta nuestros días; en los segundos, radica nuestro gusto y son reflejo de nuestra personalidad, poseen un valor material o sentimental; dotan de significado y simbolismo nuestro hogar. Ambos, son compañeros silenciosos, los cuales además, nos transportan a universos imaginarios que nos permiten recordar un viaje, un país, una cultura, una historia personal.

Como se sabe, los libros cada vez más son objetos de diseño, piezas altamente valoradas no sólo por su contenido sino por su apariencia, tipografía, color, sello editorial y otros aspectos que inclusive lo hacen alcanzar un nivel de deseo máximo para el coleccionista exigente, comparten ese valor con objetos o piezas decorativas que sin importar su origen, tamaño, temática o sus materiales se vuelven detalles que deleitan nuestra mirada. Por ello, no es casual que dentro de la decoración y el diseño de interiores, sean este par de elementos los que exijan un lugar especial desde el cual deban ser contemplados casi protagónicamente. Tomando en cuenta lo anterior, las repisas y los libreros son los elementos idóneos para satisfacer tal función, accesorios que se diseñan exclusivamente para un espacio arquitectónico y otros, que se adquieren a posteriori por sus cualidades peculiares para añadirse a un ambiente determinado.

Los libreros y repisas que contienen la fusión de estas piezas deben hacerlas lucir y al mismo tiempo engalanar un espacio, sin embargo, no puede perderse de vista que su disposición puede responder a las funciones particulares que desarrollarán: consulta y lectura frecuente; ornamento o decoración y, finalmente zonas de exhibición o protección de piezas coleccionables.

Es posible jugar con diversos materiales, formas y colores tanto como la situación lo amerite ya que su presencia puede darse en lugares diseñados integralmente con el espacio arquitectónico y ser elementos constructivos técnicamente más demandantes o por el contrario, ser completos del espacio con una sencillez mucho más precisa, casi imperceptible. Así, en conjunto con una iluminación adecuada, un espacio específico para ellos, un estilo personal para destacarlos y la creatividad o el gusto personal, son indudablemente remates visuales únicos, cargados de personalidad y carácter.

Livres et objets décoratifs font désormais partie inhérente de notre quotidien. Les premiers servent à décrire notre histoire et l'univers culturel qui nous entoure depuis l'aube des temps ; avec les derniers nous exprimons nos goûts et notre personnalité. Qu'ils aient une valeur matérielle ou sentimentale, ces objets remplissent nos foyers de sens et symbolisme. Ces compagnons silencieux nous emmènent vers des univers imaginaires ou nous rappellent des voyages, un pays, une culture, voir une anecdote personnelle.

Les livres deviennent davantage des objets d'art, des pièces très prisées, et non seulement pour le contenu, car parure, typographie, couleur et édition entrent aussi en jeu pour les rendre irrésistibles aux collectionneurs les plus exigeants. Sont également convoités les objets décoratifs qui –sans regard de la taille, la thématique ou le matériel– sauront réjouir notre regard.

Ce n'est pas un hasard si, dans l'architecture d'intérieur, ces deux éléments exigent une estrade pour prendre le devant de la scène. Les étagères et les bibliothèques sont ainsi les éléments qui remplissent aux mieux ces fonctions. Certains sont conçus exclusivement pour un espace architectural spécifique, d'autres sont acquis a posteriori pour embellir -avec ces qualités particulières- un environnement bien spécifique. Certes, les étagères et les bibliothèques doivent mettre en valeur les pièces décoratives qu'elles vont contenir, sans pour autant oublier sa fonction principale : lecture assidue, décoration ou exhibition et protection d'objets de collection.

Lorsque la fonction est définie, il convient de réunir les éléments à même de rendre une ambiance agréable. Nous pouvons jouer avec matériels, formes et couleurs, selon les circonstances de l'espace architectural, c'est-à-dire, si les meubles sont encastrables et donc avec des exigences techniques plus complexes ou bien s'ils complètent l'espace avec une simplicité beaucoup plus précise, voir même imperceptible.

Un bon éclairage, une place qui leur est consacré, un style personnel pour les mettre en avant, de la créativité et du goût personnel feront, ensemble, la touche visuelle finale chargée de personnalité et caractère.

Bücher, ebenso wie Dekorationsgegenstände, sind ein unverzichtbarer Bestandteil unseres täglichen Lebens. In ersteren befindet sich unsere Geschichte und das gesamte kulturelle Universum das uns umgibt, von der Antike bis hin zur Gegenwart. Letztere sind Ausdruck unseres Geschmacks und ein Spiegelbild unserer Persönlichkeit. Beide haben materiellen oder sentimentalen Wert und geben unserem Zuhause Bedeutung und Symbolik. Sie sind stille Begleiter, die uns in imaginäre Welten versetzen können, oder die uns an eine Reise, ein Land, eine Kultur und eine persönliche Geschichte erinnern.

Bücher werden immer mehr auch zu Designobjekten. Hoch geschätzte Stücke, die nicht nur aufgrund ihres Inhalts, sondern auch wegen ihres Aussehens, der Typografie, der Farbe und anderen Aspekten zu einem begehrten Sammlerstück anspruchsvoller Sammler werden. Diesen Wert haben auch dekorative Gegenstände, die unabhängig von ihrer Herkunft, Größe, Thematik oder Materialien unsere Augen erfreuen.

Es ist daher kein Zufall, dass in der Dekoration und Raumgestaltung diese Elemente einen zentralen Platz einnehmen. Regale und Bücherregale sind ideale Begleiter, um diese Funktion zu erfüllen. Sie werden entweder speziell für einen architektonischen Raum konzipiert oder wegen ihrer besonderen Eigenschaften nachträglich erworben, um in einer bestimmten Umgebung ihren Platz zu finden.

Regale und Bücherregale, die Bücher und Gegenstände fusionieren, sollten beide auf der einen Seite hervorheben und auf der anderen Seite mit ihnen den Raum schmücken. Deren Funktionen sollten dabei allerdings nicht in Vergessenheit geraten, wie das Lesen und der häufige Gebrauch der Bücher und der Gegenstände, die der Verzierung und der Dekoration dienen. Schließlich dienen sie auch als Ausstellungsfläche und als Schutz von Sammlerstücken. Sobald ihre Funktion festgelegt ist, können bestimmte Elemente zusammengebracht werden, die diese Komponenten auf angenehme Weise in ihre Umgebung integrieren. Man kann mit verschiedenen Materialien, Formen und Farben spielen, ganz wie es die Umstände der architektonischen Umgebung erfordern. Gleichzeitig können sie auch konstruktive und technisch anspruchsvolle Elemente sein oder die schlichte Ergänzung eines Raumes darstellen.

Zusammen mit einer entsprechenden Beleuchtung, einem für sie bestimmten Platz, gepaart mit eigenem Stil und Kreativität, sind sie zweifellos einzigartige visuelle Blickfänge, voller Persönlichkeit und Charakter.

SHELVES

REPISAS

ÉTAGÈRES

REGALE

Rustic shapes or vintage finishes help to evoke the more natural essence of these elements. In order to harmonize them as a whole, similar colors should be used in close contrast with the architectural components. Meanwhile, the objects chosen to decorate these shelves should maintain these hues, providing a homogenous appearance that agreeably frames design pieces such as clocks or lamps that draw our gaze.

Las formas rústicas o con tratamientos *vintage* nos permiten evocar la esencia más natural de estos elementos. Para armonizarlos en su conjunto se recurre a colores similares en franca relación con los componentes arquitectónicos. Por otra parte, los objetos seleccionados para decorar estas repisas conservan esas tonalidades homogenizando su apariencia enmarcando agradablemente piezas de diseño como un reloj o las luminarias que son altamente llamativos ante nuestros ojos.

Les formes rustiques ou avec des retouches vintage nous renvoient à l'essence naturelle de ces éléments. Pour créer de l'harmonie, il faut choisir des couleurs similaires et fortement liées aux composants architecturaux. Les objets choisis pour décorer les étagères doivent conserver ces couleurs afin d'encadrer les éléments de design -tels que les horloges, les luminaires- qui tant attirent notre regard.

Wenn sie eine rustikale oder Vintage Behandlung erfahren, wird ihr natürlicher Charakter hervorgehoben. Um eine Harmonie in ihrer Zusammenstellung zu erreichen, verwendet man ähnliche Farben, die sich den architektonischen Gegebenheiten anpassen. Darüber hinaus sollten die Objekte, die in den Regalen dekoriert werden, mit diesen Farbtönen korrespondieren oder ausgefallene Design Objekte wie Uhren oder Lampen unterstreichen.

The space between the steps of our staircases tends to lack any particular function, making it worthwhile converting into a set of personalized shelves that accompanies our passage and transforms this functional space into an area worthy of contemplation. Its zigzag outline generates a dynamic and pleasing form that is efficient for storing books of different sizes and formats. The contrast between materials is a common choice for emphasizing the design of the shelves as functional elements.

El espacio existente entre los peldaños de nuestras escaleras, comúnmente resulta ser un espacio sin una función determinada, por ello vale la pena convertirlo en un conjunto de repisas personalizado que acompañe nuestro recorrido y engalane este espacio funcional transformándolo en una zona digna de contemplación. Por su zigzagueante silueta el resultado es, además de dinámico, divertido y muy eficiente para almacenar libros de diversos formatos o tamaños. El contraste entre materiales es una alternativa común para realzar el diseño de las repisas como elementos funcionales.

L'espace disponible entre chacune des marches de nos escaliers ne remplie, normalement, aucune fonction, il conviendrait donc de se l'approprier pour y ajouter des étagères personnalisées pour accompagner notre parcours et transformer cet espace fonctionnel en quelque chose digne de notre regard. Grâce à sa forme en zigzag nous nous obtenons un lieu de stockage dynamique, amusant et très efficace. Le contraste des matériels est une alternative assez utilisée pour mettre en valeur le design de ces objets hautement fonctionnels.

Der Raum zwischen den Sprossen der Treppe, ist gemeinhin ein Raum ohne eine bestimmte Funktion. Daher lohnt es sich, diesen Raum mit einem maßgeschneiderten Regal zu ergänzen, dass ihn in einen funktionalen und ansprechenden Bereich umwandelt. Eine Zickzackform macht das Regal dynamisch, heiter und sehr effizient, um dort Bücher in verschiedenen Formaten und Größen aufzubewahren. Der Kontrast zwischen den Materialien ist eine gängige Möglichkeit, das Design dieser Regale zu unterstreichen.

living areas

zonas de estar

salles de séjour

wohnbereiche

Arranging books horizontally on low shelves is a surefire method of drawing attention to this space without oversaturating it.

La colocación horizontal de libros en repisas de baja altura es una forma muy acertada para hacer lucir este espacio sin saturarlo.

Placer les livres en horizontal et sur des étagères à basse hauteur est une bonne manière de mettre en valeur cet espace sans le saturer.

Die horizontale Anordnung von Büchern in Regalen geringer Höhe ist eine sehr empfehlenswerte Art, um sie zur Geltung zu bringen ohne dass es überladen wirkt.

To achieve a more welcoming appearance, vases, sculptures and picture frames are combined. Books do not always need to be the principal objects in these spaces.

Para obtener una apariencia más acogedora se fusionan floreros, esculturas y portarretratos. No siempre los libros necesitan ser los protagonistas de estos espacios.

Pour davantage de chaleur, ajoutez-y des vases et des portraits. Les livres ne doivent pas toujours les protagonistes de ces espaces.

Um eine gemütlichere Atmosphäre zu schaffen, kombiniert man Vasen, Skulpturen und Bilder miteinander. Bücher müssen nicht immer die Protagonisten dieser Räume sein.

Living spaces are the ideal zones
to contemplate and put on dis-
play pieces that form part of
our collections, without putting
their completeness at risk.

Las zonas de estar son el espacio idóneo para contemplar y
exhibir piezas que formen parte
de nuestras colecciones sin poner
en riesgo su integridad.

Les salles de séjours sont les
endroits idéaux pour exposer et
admirer les objets de collection
sans mettre en péril leur intégrité.

Wohnbereiche sind der ideale
Ort, um Sammlerstücke auszu
stellen ohne ihre Integrität
zu verletzen.

Lighting and the materials used in the construction process play an important role in highlighting the beauty of the objects they hold.

La iluminación y los materiales empleados en el proceso constructivo juegan un papel importante para destacar la belleza de los objetos que albergan.

L'éclairage et les matériels dans la construction jouent un rôle primordial pour mettre en avant la beauté des objets qu'ils contiennent.

Die Beleuchtung und Materialien, die beim Bau verwendet werden sind wichtig, um die Schönheit der Objekte, die sie beherbergen hervorzuheben.

Avoiding visual saturation can help smaller spaces to appear clean and impeccable, with a refined elegance.

Evitar la saturación visual puede favorecer a que los espacios más pequeños se perciban limpios o impecables, con una elegancia depurada.

Evitez la saturation visuelle dans les espaces plus petits afin de rendre une image propre, d'une élégance épurée.

Wenn man eine visuelle Sättigung vermeidet, erreicht man, dass kleinere Räume als ordentlich, sauber und raffiniert elegant empfunden werden.

It should not be forgotten that shelves go hand in hand with the design of the architectural space, condensing the style or combination of objects that this contains.

No puede perderse de vista que las repisas mantienen concordancia con el diseño del espacio arquitectónico, condensan el estilo o la mezcla de objetos que el primero posee.

N'oubliez pas que les étagères doivent accompagner le design de l'espace architectural, puisqu'elles condensent le style ou le mélange d'objets de ce premier.

Wichtig ist auch, dass die Regale im Einklang mit der Gestaltung des architektonischen Raums stehen und dass sie dessen Stil oder die Mischung von Objekten, die er beherbergt unterstreichen.

bedrooms & bathrooms

dormitorios y baños

chambres et salles de bain

schlafzimmer und bäder

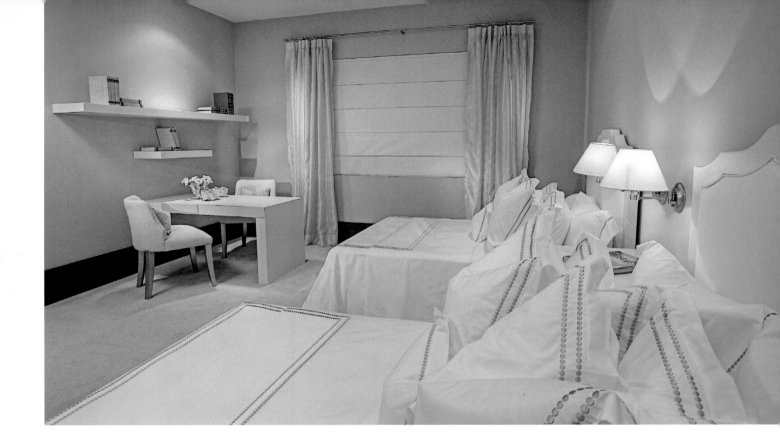

The formal simplicity of shelving makes it easier to alter its design to match the season, using only color and shape.

La sencillez formal de las repisas puede contribuir a cambiar su diseño con mayor facilidad para dotarlos de temporalidad, empleando sólo el uso del color y la forma.

La simplicité des étagères permet de changer de design assez facilement pour être à jour avec la saison, il suffit de jouer un peu avec la couleur et la forme.

Die formale Schlichtheit von Regalen macht es möglich, ihr Design leicht zu verändern und sie farblich und ihre Form zeitgemäß zu gestalten.

In a private space for relaxation it is important that order and balance are always to the fore, since oversaturation can be enervating.

En un espacio íntimo o de descanso, el orden y el equilibrio deben imperar en todo momento, la saturación puede ser poco reconfortante.

Dans un espace intime ou consacré au repos, l'ordre et l'équilibre doivent régner à tout moment, la saturation peut s'avérer peu satisfaisante.

In einem intimen Raum, der der Entspannung dient, sollten stets Ordnung und Gleichgewicht herrschen. Ist er zu übersättigt, kann das zu einem unbehaglichen Gefühl führen.

The color of the shelving used for shoes and clothing can add a touch of fun and enjoyment, while remaining elegant.

Gracias al color que pueden albergar las repisas destinadas para el calzado o la vestimenta, éstas pueden tener un toque divertido y jovial sin dejar de ser elegantes.

La couleur des étagères pour les chaussures et les habits peut ajouter une touche d'amusement et de joie, tout en étant élégantes.

Die Farben von Schuhregalen oder Kleiderregalen geben diesen eine unterhaltsame und fröhliche Note, während sie aber gleichzeitig auch elegant wirken können.

Only essential items should be placed in a bathroom, above all when the shelves are designed to match the wall finishings or the accessories.

En una sala de baño se coloca lo esencial, sobre todo cuando las repisas se han diseñado para mimetizarse con los acabados de muros o accesorios.

Dans une salle de bains il ne doit y avoir que ce qui est essentiel, surtout si elles ont été conçues pour rappeler les finitions des murs ou des accessoires.

In einem Badezimmer bewahrt man das Wesentliche auf, insbesondere dann wenn die Regale dazu entworfen wurden, um mit den Oberflächen der Wände und Accessoires zu korrespondieren.

BOOKCASES

LIBREROS
BIBLIOTHÈQUES
BÜCHERREGALE

Bookshelves can in themselves be the focus of attention in a room. With their size, design, material or contents, they are often compared to murals that change over time and through the frequency of their use, or canvases painted with the colors of the books. Functionally, it is recommended that those books most often consulted are placed at an accessible height.

Los libreros son en sí mismos espacios protagónicos que pueden ser el foco de atención de nuestra mirada. Por su tamaño, diseño, materialidad o contenido, estos en muchas ocasiones se han comparado con murales pictóricos que tienen la cualidad de cambiar con el tiempo y su frecuencia de uso, lienzos que se pintan con el color de sus libros. Funcionalmente se recomienda que su diseño permita tener a una altura accesible aquellos que con frecuencia consultamos.

Les étagères à livres peuvent être ces vedettes qui attirent notre regard. La taille, le design, le matériel ou le contenu peut rappeler une fresque qui change avec le temps y la fréquence de son utilisation, les livres sont les canevas avec lesquels nous créons des images. Le design devrait rendre accessible les livres que nous lisons fréquemment.

Bücherregale selbst sind Einrichtungsgegenstände, die im Mittelpunkt unserer Aufmerksamkeit stehen können. Aufgrund ihrer Größe, ihres Designs, ihres Materials oder ihres Inhalts, wurden sie schon oft mit Wandmalereien verglichen, die sich im Laufe der Zeit verändern und durch die Farben der Bücher bemalt erscheinen. Die Bücher, die oft gelesen werden, sollten auf einer gut zugänglichen Höhe aufgestellt werden.

A good bookshelf can be complemented by two principal elements: a large-scale work of art to decorate this space; and a reading corner for spending long sessions that are a pleasure for both mind and body. In this way the space can take the lead in cultivating private reflection without becoming boring or lacking personality. This will make it a charming spot and a delight for the eye.

Un buen librero puede complementarse con dos elementos de privilegio: una obra de arte en gran formato que engalane este espacio y una zona de lectura que permita pasar largas sesiones confortables y placenteras a nivel físico pero también intelectual. De este modo este espacio adquiere una dimensión privilegiada que favorece la reflexión íntima sin convertiste en un espacio aburrido falto de personalidad. El resultado es seductor y agradable a la mirada.

Une bonne étagère à livres peut être complétée par deux éléments privilégiés: une œuvre d'art en grand format qui va décorer cet espace; un coin lecture pour des longues séances en tout confort et joie, physiques et intellectuels. Cet espace va ainsi prendre le devant pour favoriser la plus profonde réflexion, l'ennui et le manque de personnalité n'ont pas lieu d'exister. Voici un endroit charmant et qui réjoui le regard.

Ein gutes Bücherregal kann durch Elemente ergänzt werden, z. B. durch ein Kunstwerk in Großformat, das diesen Raum verziert und eine Leseecke, in der man sich gerne länger gemütlich lesend aufhält. Dadurch bekommt der Raum eine sehr persönliche und schöne Note und lädt zum Nachdenken ein. Das Ergebnis einer derartigen Gestaltung ist gleichzeitig verführerisch wie auch schön anzusehen.

studies
estudios
bureaux
studios

The colors or materials used in the design and manufacture of a bookshelf make it possible to create contrast with the architectural space. It matters little whether the decoration is uniform or heterogeneous: the charm does not depend on this combination.

Por los colores o materiales con los que se diseña y fabrica un librero, es posible contrastar adecuadamente los espacios arquitectónicos con la decoración, uniforme o heterogénea la combinación no demerita su encanto.

Grâce aux couleurs et matériels d'une bibliothèque, nous pouvons contraster les espaces architecturaux. Peu importe si la décoration est uniforme ou hétérogène, le charme ne dépend pas de cette combinaison.

Durch Farben oder Materialien, mit denen ein Bücherregal gestaltet wird, kann man einen passenden Kontrast zur Architektur herstellen. Eine einheitliche oder heterogene Dekoration kann dies sogar unterstreichen.

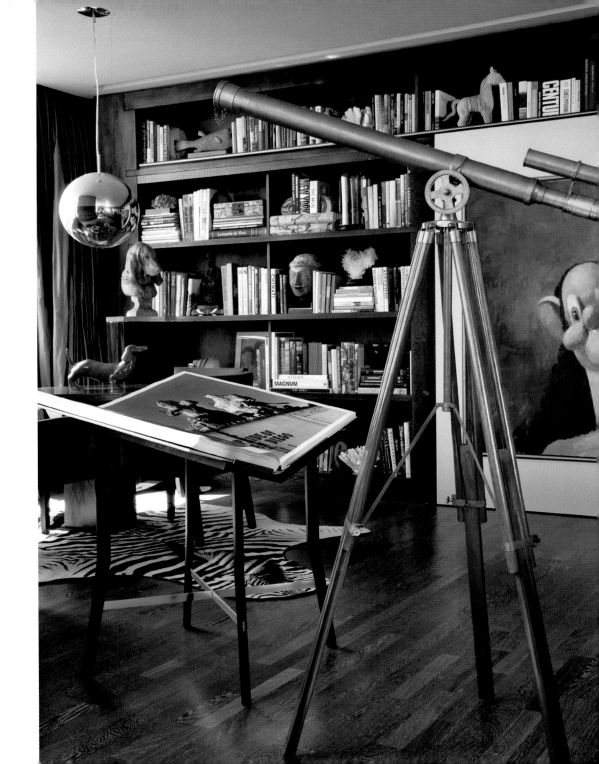

It is advisable to take an informal approach to the arrangement of objects, in order to achieve a dynamic and lively space that is more casual in appearance.

Es recomendable emplear un manejo informal en la disposición de los objetos con el fin de lograr un espacio dinámico y vivo, más casual en su apariencia.

Il convient d'arranger les objets de façon informelle afin de recréer un espace dynamique et vivant, avec un aire informel.

Es ist ratsam, die Objekte informell anzuordnen, um einen dynamischen und lebendigen Raum mit einer entspannten Atmosphäre zu schaffen.

Using a background color for your bookshelf is an excellent way of emphasizing its features. It is also possible to use it as a screen to visually divide a space.

Usar un color de fondo para nuestro librero es altamente recomendable para destacar sus atributos. También es posible emplearlo como celosía para dividir visualmente un espacio.

Nous vous conseillons d'utiliser une couleur de fond avec la bibliothèque si vous souhaitez de mettre en avant ses qualités. Nous pouvons également nous en servir comme cloison pour diviser un espace.

Es wird dringend empfohlen, eine Hintergrundfarbe für Bücherregale zu verwenden, um ihre Eigenschaften hervorzuheben. Mann kann ein Regal auch als Raumteiler verwenden.

libraries

bibliotecas

bibliothèques

bibliotheken

A bookcase is an intimate reflection of the inhabitants of a house: its geometry, design, material and the volumes it holds ascribe warmth, harmony and dynamism to the interior architecture.

Una biblioteca es un reflejo íntimo de los moradores de un espacio residencial: su geometría, diseño, materiales y, los volúmenes que alberga, otorga calidez, armonía y dinamismo a la arquitectura interior.

Une bibliothèque est un reflet intime de l'habitant: géométrie, design, matériaux et volumes, apportent une touche de chaleur, harmonie et dynamisme à l'architecture d'intérieur.

Eine Bibliothek sagt viel über den Bewohner eines Wohnraumes aus. Aber die Geometrie, das Design, das Material und die Anzahl der Regale, die sie beherbergt verleihen dem Raum Wärme, Harmonie und Dynamik.

Rear lighting works perfectly
when a bookcase forms part of
a niche. Bathed in light, it be-
comes a very elegant focal point.

La iluminación posterior funcio-
na a la perfección cuando un
librero forma parte de un nicho
arquitectónico, el baño de luz
puede convertiste en un detalle
muy elegante.

L'éclairage est la touche
parfaite sin pour une bibliothèque encastrable. Le bain de
lumière peut s'avérer être un
détail très élégant.

Die Hintergrundbeleuchtung
funktioniert perfekt, wenn ein
Bücherregal Teil einer architektonischen Nische ist, wenn diese
in Licht getaucht wird, kann das
ein elegantes Detail darstellen.

MENU:
- Pimientos rellenos
  de cordero
- Crema de alcachofa
- Ceviche peruano
- robalo a la sal

Ingredientes
6 pimientos rojos
400 gr cordero
6 alcachofas
500 gr Robalo
1 kg. Sal de mar

There are no precise rules for making these elements stand out; however one of the most frequent is to place them in double-height spaces, rendering them more contemplative and distinguished.

No existen reglas precisas para hacer lucir estos elementos, pese a ello una de las más comunes es incorporarlos a espacios a doble altura, volviéndolos más contemplativos y distinguidos.

Il n'y a pas de formule unique pour mette en valeur ces éléments. Les espaces sur une double hauteur les rendent plus contemplatifs et distingués.

Es gibt keine genauen Regeln, um diese Elemente hervorzuheben, jedoch eine der häufigsten ist es, sie in Räumen von doppelter Höhe zu integrieren, so, dass sie kontemplativer und exklusiver wirken.

The presence of a bookcase is essential to converting a cold space
into a welcoming one. Every home
should probably include one, no
matter its size.

La presencia de libreros es funda-
mental para convertir un espacio
frío en uno abrigador. Podría
considerarse que cada casa debe
incorporar un librero sin importar
su escala.

Leur seule présence peut rendre
un espace froid en un coin cha-
leureux. Peut importe l'échelle,
chaque maison devrait en avoir un.

Ihre Anwesenheit ist unerlässlich,
um einen kalten in einen ge-
mütlichen Raum umzugestalten.
Jedes Haus sollte mindestens ein
Bücherregal sein eigen nennen,
unabhängig von seiner Größe.

184-185 Paola Calzada | **187** Fernando de Haro, Jesús Fernández, Omar Fuentes & Bertha Figueroa | **188** José M. Nogal Moragues | **189** Olga Hanono & Sarah Mizrahi | **190-191** Fred Dionne | **192** Fernando de Haro, Jesús Fernández, Omar Fuentes & Bertha Figueroa | **193** Paola Aboumrad | **196** David Penjos | **198-199** Fernando de Haro, Jesús Fernández, Omar Fuentes & Bertha Figueroa | **202** Mariangel Coghlan | **205** José Lew & Bernardo Lew | **206** Carlos Magaña & Mauricio Magaña | **207** Blanca González, Maribel González & Mely González | **209** Olga Hanono & Sarah Mizrahi | **210** Fernando de Haro, Jesús Fernández, Omar Fuentes, Bertha Figueroa & Jorge Torres | **211** Mariangel Álvarez & Covadonga Hernández | **213** Blanca González, Maribel González & Mely González | **218-219** Gerardo García | **222-223** Ulises Castañeda | **224-225** Genaro Nieto | **226-227** Alejandra Prieto, Cecilia Prieto & Claudia Ortega | **228-229** Olga Hanono & Sarah Mizrahi | **230-231** Covadonga Hernández | **234-235** Covadonga Hernández | **236-237** José Lew & Bernardo Lew | **240-241** Blanca González, Maribel González & Mely González | **248** Gerardo Broissin, Mauricio Cristóbal, Rodrigo Jiménez & Alejandro Rocha | **249** Enrique Bardasano, Diego Bardasano & Andrés Bardasano | **250-251** Javier Valenzuela & Fernando Valenzuela | **256** Ezequiel Farca | **257** Miguel Ochoa Anaya | **258-259** Covadonga Hernández | **262** Olga Hanono & Sarah Mizrahi | **263** Covadonga Hernández | **268-269** Fernando de Haro, Jesús Fernández, Omar Fuentes & Bertha Figueroa | **273** Robert Duarte & Vanessa Patiño | **274-275** Gilberto L. Rodríguez | **279** Elías Kababie

FOTÓGRAFOS PHOTOGRAPHES FOTOGRAFEN

PHOTOGRAPHERS

Editado en Octubre de 2013. Impreso en China.
El cuidado de edición estuvo a cargo de
AM Editores S.A. de C.V.
Edited in October 2013. Printed in China.
Published by AM Editores S.A. de C.V.